T0322182

Master Maths at Home

Multiplication and Division

Scan the QR code to help
your child's learning at home.

DK | MATHS
NO PROBLEM!

mastermathsathome.com

How to use this book

Maths — No Problem! created **Master Maths at Home** to help children develop fluency in the subject and a rich understanding of core concepts.

Key features of the Master Maths at Home books include:

- Carefully designed lessons that provide structure, but also allow flexibility in how they're used.

- Speech bubbles containing content designed to spark diverse conversations, with many discussion points that don't have obvious 'right' or 'wrong' answers.

- Rich illustrations that will guide children to a discussion of shapes and units of measurement, allowing them to make connections to the wider world around them.

- Exercises that allow a flexible approach and can be adapted to suit any child's cognitive or functional ability.

- Clearly laid-out pages that encourage children to practise a range of higher-order skills.

- A community of friendly and relatable characters who introduce each lesson and come along as your child progresses through the series.

You can see more guidance on how to use these books at **mastermathsathome.com**.

We're excited to share all the ways you can learn maths!

Copyright © 2022 Maths — No Problem!

Maths — No Problem!
mastermathsathome.com
www.mathsnoproblem.com
hello@mathsnoproblem.com

First published in Great Britain in 2022 by
Dorling Kindersley Limited
One Embassy Gardens, 8 Viaduct Gardens, London SW11 7BW
A Penguin Random House Company

The authorised representative in the EEA is Dorling Kindersley
Verlag GmbH. Amulfstr. 124, 80636 Munich, Germany

10 9 8 7 6 5 4 3 2 1
001–327083–Jan/22

A CIP catalogue record for this book is available from the British Library.

ISBN: 978-0-24153-925-5
Printed and bound in the UK

For the curious
www.dk.com

This book was made with Forest Stewardship Council™ certified paper – one small step in DK's commitment to a sustainable future. For more information go to www.dk.com/our-green-pledge

Acknowledgements
The publisher would like to thank the authors and consultants Andy Psarianos, Judy Hornigold, Adam Gifford and Dr Anne Hermanson.

The Castledown typeface has been used with permission from the Colophon Foundry.

Contents

Ruby   Elliott   Amira   Charles   Lulu   Sam   Oak   Holly   Ravi   Emma   Jacob   Hannah

Multiplying by 3

Starter

Amira makes this shape using lolly sticks. How many lolly sticks will Amira need to make 6 of the shapes?

Example

Each shape is made with 3 lolly sticks.

1 group of 3
$1 \times 3 = 3$

2 groups of 3
$2 \times 3 = 6$

3 groups of 3
$3 \times 3 = 9$

4 groups of 3
$4 \times 3 = 12$

5 groups of 3
$5 \times 3 = 15$

6 groups of 3
$6 \times 3 = 18$

I can use a number line to count in threes.

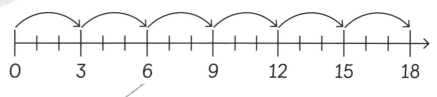

0   3   6   9   12   15   18

I can use counters to help me. I can arrange them like this. 6 rows of 3 makes 18.

Amira will need 18 lolly sticks to make 6 of the shapes.

Practice

1 Fill in the blanks.

(a)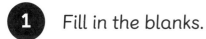

3 × 2 = ☐

3 × 4 = ☐

(b)

3 × 3 = ☐

(c)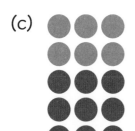

3 × ☐ = ☐

2 Draw lines to match.

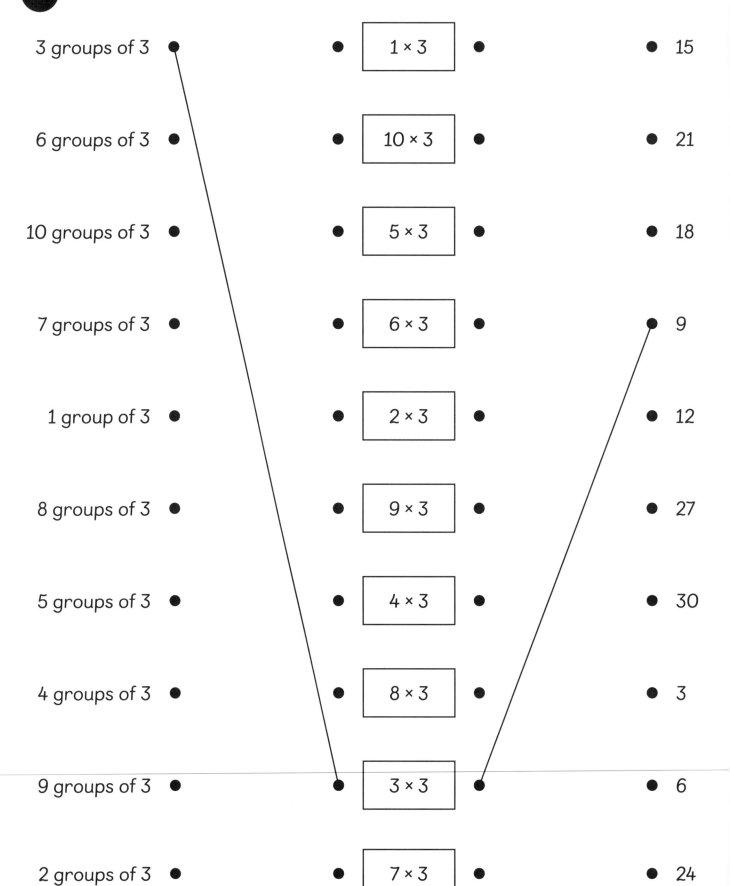

3 groups of 3 •

6 groups of 3 •

10 groups of 3 •

7 groups of 3 •

1 group of 3 •

8 groups of 3 •

5 groups of 3 •

4 groups of 3 •

9 groups of 3 •

2 groups of 3 •

• | 1 × 3 | •

• | 10 × 3 | •

• | 5 × 3 | •

• | 6 × 3 | •

• | 2 × 3 | •

• | 9 × 3 | •

• | 4 × 3 | •

• | 8 × 3 | •

• | 3 × 3 | •

• | 7 × 3 | •

• 15

• 21

• 18

• 9

• 12

• 27

• 30

• 3

• 6

• 24

3 The baker bakes bread in batches of 3 loaves at a time.
He bakes 4 batches in the morning. He then bakes 5 batches in the afternoon.

morning | 3 | 3 | 3 | 3 |

afternoon | 3 | 3 | 3 | 3 | 3 |

(a) How many loaves does he bake in the morning?

The baker bakes ☐ loaves in the morning.

(b) How many loaves does he bake in the afternoon?

The baker bakes ☐ loaves in the afternoon.

(c) How many loaves does he bake altogether?

The baker bakes ☐ loaves altogether.

Multiplying by 4

Starter

How many peaches does the grocer have for sale?

Example

I can count in fours. Each punnet has 4 peaches.

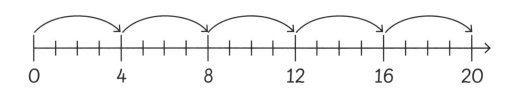

Each punnet is a group of 4 peaches. There are 5 groups of 4.
5 × 4 = 20

The grocer has 20 peaches for sale.

1 Fill in the blanks.

(a)  $1 \times 4 = 4$

(b) ⠿⠿ $2 \times 4 = \boxed{}$

(c) ⠿⠿⠿ $3 \times 4 = \boxed{}$

(d) ⠿⠿⠿⠿ $\boxed{} \times 4 = \boxed{}$

(e) ⠿⠿⠿⠿⠿ $\boxed{} \times 4 = \boxed{}$

(f) ⠿⠿⠿⠿⠿⠿ $\boxed{} \times 4 = \boxed{}$

(g) ⠿⠿⠿⠿⠿⠿⠿ $\boxed{} \times 4 = \boxed{}$

(h) ⠿⠿⠿⠿⠿⠿⠿⠿ $\boxed{} \times 4 = \boxed{}$

(i) ⠿⠿⠿⠿⠿⠿⠿⠿⠿ $\boxed{} \times \boxed{} = \boxed{}$

(j) ⠿⠿⠿⠿⠿⠿⠿⠿⠿⠿ $\boxed{} \times \boxed{} = \boxed{}$

2 How many drinks are there altogether?

$4 \times \boxed{} = \boxed{}$

There are $\boxed{}$ drinks altogether.

3 A pack of kitchen rolls has 6 rolls in it.
How many kitchen rolls are there in 4 packs?

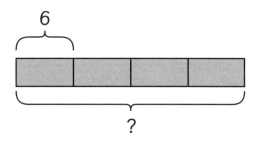

There are $\boxed{}$ kitchen rolls in 4 packs.

4 Elliott has 4 times as many pencils as Emma. Emma has 5 pencils. How many pencils does Elliott have?

5

Emma

Elliott

?

Elliott has ☐ pencils.

5 Solve and fill in the blanks.
Last term Sam read 2 books. Lulu read 3 times as many books as Sam read.

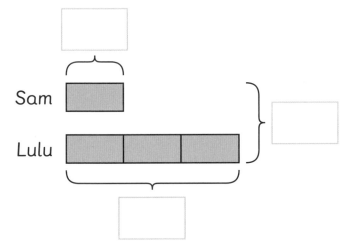

Sam

Lulu

How many books in total did Sam and Lulu read last term?

☐ × 4 = ☐

Sam and Lulu read ☐ books in total last term.

Multiplying by 8

Starter

How many counters are there?

Example

Each row has 4 red counters and 4 blue counters.

1 × 4 = 4	1 × 8 = 8
2 × 4 = 8	2 × 8 = 16
3 × 4 = 12	3 × 8 = 24
4 × 4 = 16	4 × 8 = 32
5 × 4 = 20	5 × 8 = 40

There are 40 counters.

1 Fill in the blanks.

(a) 4 × 8 = ☐

(b) 3 × 8 = ☐

(c) ☐ × 8 = 8

(d) 5 × 8 = ☐

(e) 8 × 8 = ☐

(f) 8 × 10 = ☐

(g) ☐ × 8 = 56

(h) 9 × 8 = ☐

(i) 2 × 8 = ☐

(j) ☐ × 8 = 48

2 Match.

| 8 × 5 | ● | | ● | 32 |

| 3 × 8 | ● | | ● | 6 × 4 |

| 64 | ● | | ● | 8 × 8 |

| 4 × 8 | ● | | ● | 4 × 10 |

Dividing by 3

Starter

Charles is putting the tennis balls into containers to put them away.

How many containers does Charles need?

Example

There are 24
tennis balls to put away.
Each container can hold
3 tennis balls.

We need to divide
24 by 3 to find how many
containers we need.
24 ÷ 3 = 8

Charles needs 8 containers to put the tennis balls away.

1 (a) Circle the counters to show groups of 3 and fill in the blanks.

☐ ÷ 3 = ☐

There are ☐ groups of 3 counters.

(b) Circle the stars to show 3 equal groups and fill in the blanks.

☐ ÷ 3 = ☐

There are ☐ stars in each group.

2 Divide and fill in the blanks.

(a) $21 \div 3 =$ ☐

(b) $15 \div 3 =$ ☐

(c) ☐ $\div 3 = 10$

(d) ☐ $\div 3 = 6$

3 Oak has 24 doughnuts to put on plates for her party. Each plate should have 3 doughnuts. How many plates does Oak need?

Oak needs ☐ plates.

4 A roll of fabric is 27 m long. It needs to be cut into 3 pieces of equal length. How long will each piece be?

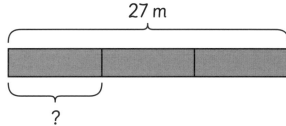

27 m

?

Each piece of fabric will be ☐ m long.

Dividing by 4

Starter

The children want to share the box of chocolates equally.

How many chocolates does each child get?

Example

There are 12 chocolates in the box.

We need to divide 12 by 4.
12 ÷ 4 = 3

Each child gets 3 chocolates.

1 Circle the counters to show 4 equal groups and fill in the blanks.

$\boxed{} \div 4 = \boxed{}$

There are $\boxed{}$ equal groups.

2 Circle to show groups of 4 counters and fill in the blanks.

$\boxed{} \div 4 = \boxed{}$

There are $\boxed{}$ groups of 4 counters.

3 Fill in the blanks.

(a) $16 \div 4 = \boxed{}$ (b) $12 \div 4 = \boxed{}$

(c) $36 \div 4 = \boxed{}$ (d) $\boxed{} \div 4 = 6$

(e) $28 \div 4 = \boxed{}$ (f) $\boxed{} \div 4 = 8$

4 Four children share 8 slices of pizza equally.
How much pizza does each child get?

8

Each child gets [ ] slices of pizza.

5 Charles and his friends need to set up tables with 4 chairs
each for the school picnic.
There are 32 chairs in total.
How many tables can they set up?

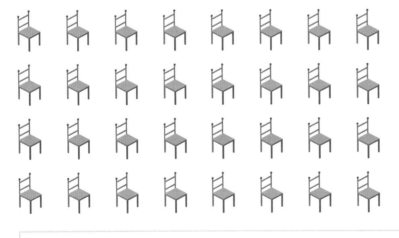

Charles and his friends can set up [ ] tables with 4 chairs each.

6 Together, Emma and Ravi scored 40 points in a game.
Emma scored 3 times as many points as Ravi scored.
How many points did Ravi score?

Emma ⬚⬚⬚ }
Ravi ⬚ } 40

Ravi scored ⬚ points.

7 Elliott grew 36 tomato plants from seeds.
He gave some of his tomato plants to Oak.
Elliott now has 3 times as many tomato plants as Oak.
How many tomato plants did he give to Oak?

Elliott gave Oak ⬚ tomato plants.

Dividing by 8

Starter

Hannah and Elliott need 40 drinks for the school picnic.
The drinks come in packs of 8.

How many packs of drinks do they need to buy?

Example

We need to divide to find out how many packs are needed.

Each pack has 8 drinks.
$40 \div 8 = 5$

Fruit Drinks 8 Pack

Hannah and Elliott need to buy 5 packs for the school picnic.

Practice

1 Circle to show groups of 8 counters and fill in the blanks.

$\boxed{} \div 8 = \boxed{}$

There are $\boxed{}$ groups of 8 counters.

2 Circle the counters to show 8 equal groups and fill in the blanks.

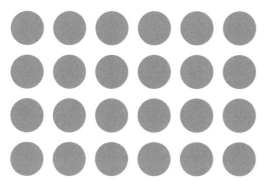

$\boxed{} \div 8 = \boxed{}$

There are $\boxed{}$ counters in each group.

3 Fill in the blanks.

(a) $8 \div 8 = \boxed{}$

(b) $24 \div 8 = \boxed{}$

(c) $64 \div 8 = \boxed{}$

(d) $32 \div 8 = \boxed{}$

(e) $16 \div 8 = \boxed{}$

(f) $72 \div 8 = \boxed{}$

(g) $40 \div 8 = \boxed{}$

(h) $\boxed{} \div 8 = 6$

(i) $\boxed{} \div 8 = 10$

(j) $\boxed{} \div 8 = 7$

4 A card game uses 48 playing cards. Each of the 8 players gets an equal number of cards.
How many cards does each player get?

48

Each player gets [ ] cards.

5 A school has bought 56 new books. The children need 8 books to fill 1 shelf in the library. How many shelves can the children fill with new books?

The children can fill [ ] shelves with new books.

6 Ravi has 1 pack of trading cards, Ruby has 3 packs of trading cards and Elliott has 4 packs of trading cards. In total, there are 80 cards. Each pack has the same number of cards.
How many cards are in each pack of trading cards?

Ravi

Ruby   } 80

Elliott

There are [ ] cards in each pack of trading cards.

7 Emma's cousin has 72 guests coming to her wedding reception.
Emma needs to help set the tables for 8 guests each.
How many tables does she need to set?

Emma needs to set [ ] tables.

Multiplying 2-digit numbers

Starter

How many eggs does the farmer have for sale?

Example

Each carton has 1 dozen eggs. There are 4 cartons.

1 dozen is equal to 12.

We can split 12 into 1 ten and 2 ones.

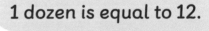

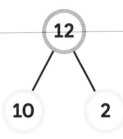

12

10   2

We can multiply the ones.
2 × 4 = 8

Next we can multiply the tens.
10 × 4 = 40

Now we add the ones and the tens.
8 + 40 = 48

The farmer has 48 eggs for sale.

Practice

Solve and fill in the blanks.

1   21 × 4 = ☐   21

1

2   43 × 2 = ☐   43

3

3   32 × 3 = ☐   32

2

4   23 × 2 = ☐   23

3

5   13 × 4 = ☐   13

3

6   34 × 4 = ☐   34

4

Multiplying with renaming

Starter

Emma designed labels on a computer for the preserves
she made with her aunt. Emma printed 7 sheets.
There are 36 labels on each sheet.

How many labels has she printed?

Example

Each sheet has
36 labels. There are
7 sheets of labels.

36 × 7 = ?

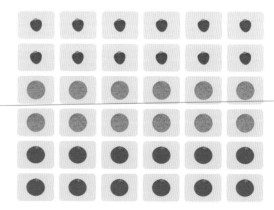

Method 1

Step 1 Multiply the ones by 7.

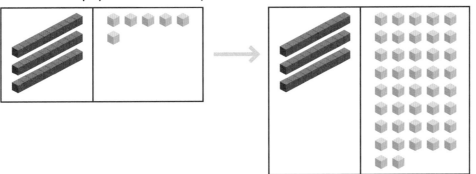

Step 2 Rename the ones.

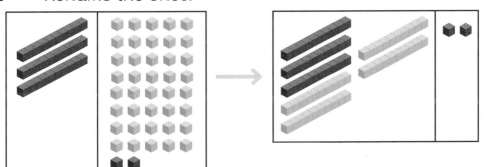

42 ones = 4 tens and 2 ones

	t	o
	3	6
×		7
	4	2

Step 3 Multiply the tens by 7.

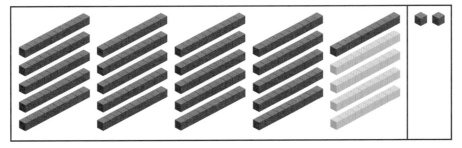

3 tens × 7 = 21 tens

	h	t	o
		3	6
×			7
		4	2
	2	1	0

Step 4 Add the products.

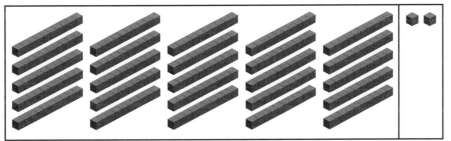

42 + 210 = 252

36 × 7 = 252

	h	t	o
		3	6
×			7
		4	2
+	2	1	0
	2	5	2

Method 2

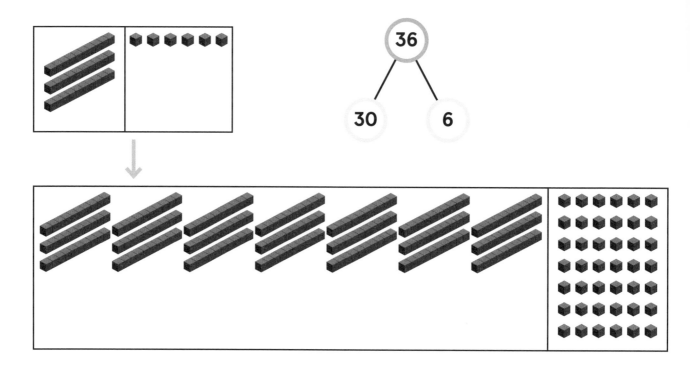

Step 1   Multiply the ones.

6 ones × 7 = 42 ones

42 ones = 4 tens + 2 ones

	t	o
4 tens ⟩ ⁴		
	3	6
×		7
		2 ⟨ 2 ones

Step 2   Multiply the tens.

3 tens × 7 = 21 tens

21 tens + 4 tens = 25 tens

25 tens + 2 ones = 252

36 × 7 = 252

	h	t	o
		⁴ 3	6
×			7
	2	5	2

25 tens = 2 hundreds + 5 tens

Emma printed 252 labels.

Practice

1 Multiply.

(a)

h	t	o
	3	6
×		3

□ □ □

(b)

h	t	o
	7	2
×		4

□ □ □

(c)

h	t	o
	2	4
×		7

□ □ □

(d)

h	t	o
	4	6
×		3

□ □ □

(e)

h	t	o
	4	8
×		8

□ □ □

(f)

h	t	o
	8	6
×		7

□ □ □

2 Lulu swam 9 lengths of a swimming pool.
The swimming pool is 25 m long.
How many metres did Lulu swim in total?

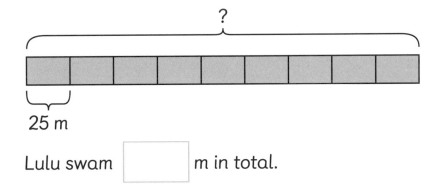

Lulu swam ☐ m in total.

Dividing 2-digit numbers

Starter

Emma and Charles want to share
their cards equally to play a game.
There are 64 cards.
How many cards does each player get?

Example

We can split
64 into 60 and 4 and
then divide them by 2.
$60 \div 2 = 30$
$4 \div 2 = 2$

64

60   4

We can then add
the two quotients to
find the answer.
$30 + 2 = 32$

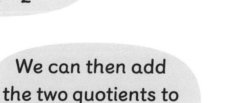

A quotient is
the result when we
divide one number
by another.

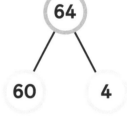

Each player gets 32 cards.

Practice

Solve and fill in the blanks.

1 69 ÷ 3 = ☐

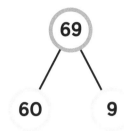

2 48 ÷ 2 = ☐

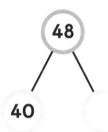

3 96 ÷ 3 = ☐

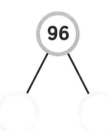

4 84 ÷ 4 = ☐

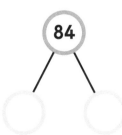

Dividing with renaming

Starter

How can Jacob and Elliott divide 51 by 3?

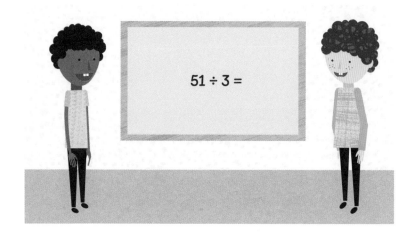

$51 \div 3 =$

Example

I tried splitting 51 into 50 and 1 but it didn't help.

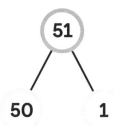

51

50   1

Maybe there is a better way to split 51.

Can we split 51 into 30 and 21? Both 30 and 21 are easy to divide by 3.

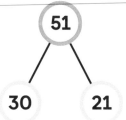

51

30   21

Practice

Solve and fill in the blanks.

1   64 ÷ 4 = ⬚

2   70 ÷ 5 = ⬚

3   81 ÷ 3 = ⬚

4   96 ÷ 6 = ⬚

Dividing using long division

Starter

This way of dividing is called **long division**.

How does long division work?

Example

I can see that we also split 51 into 30 and 21 but it is written in a different way.

Doing it this way shows all of the steps.

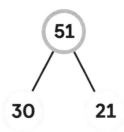

51

30   21

```
        1   7
3 )     5   1
    −   3   0
        2   1
    −   2   1
            0
```

Step 1 Take 30 from 51.
Step 2 Take 21 from 21.

30 tens ÷ 3 = 1 ten

1 ten   7 ones

```
        1   7
3 )     5   1
    −   3   0
        2   1
    −   2   1
            0
```

21 ones ÷ 3 = 7 ones

1 ten + 7 ones = 17
51 ÷ 3 = 17

There is another way.
It is called **short division**.

short division

```
      1   7
3 )   5  ₂1
```

long division

```
        1   7
3 )     5   1
    −   3   0
        2   1
    −   2   1
            0
```

Short division has the same
steps as long division but we
don't write it all down.

Solve and fill in the blanks.

1 72 ÷ 3 = ⬜

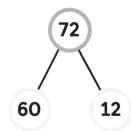

```
        2   ⬜
    3 ) 7   2
      - 6   0
    ─────────
        1   2
    -  ⬜  ⬜
    ─────────
            0
```

2 76 ÷ 2 = ⬜

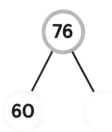

```
        3   ⬜
    2 ) 7   6
      - 6   0
    ─────────
       ⬜  ⬜
    -  ⬜  ⬜
    ─────────
            0
```

3 85 ÷ 5 = ⬜

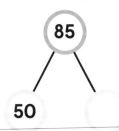

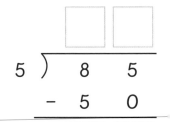

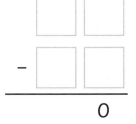

```
       ⬜  ⬜
    5 ) 8   5
      - 5   0
    ─────────
       ⬜  ⬜
    -  ⬜  ⬜
    ─────────
            0
```

4　$87 \div 3 =$ [　　　]

```
        ┌─┐ ┌─┐
     ┌──┤ │ │ │
   3 )   8   7
     ─ ┌─┐ ┌─┐
       │ │ │ │
       └─┘ └─┘
       ┌─┐ ┌─┐
       │ │ │ │
       └─┘ └─┘
     ─ ┌─┐ ┌─┐
       │ │ │ │
       └─┘ └─┘
            0
```

5　Sam's father is 45 years old. He is 5 times older than Sam and 9 times older than Sam's brother.
How old are Sam and his brother?

Sam is [　　] years old and his brother is [　　] years old.

Dividing using short division

Starter

A florist needs to put all the flowers into 5 vases so that each vase has the same amount of flowers.

How many flowers should he put in each vase?

75 ☀

Example

Ravi's method

There are 75 flowers in the box. I can split 75 into 50 and 25.

$50 \div 5 = 10$ $25 \div 5 = 5$
We then add the 2 quotients together.
$10 + 5 = 15$.

75

50   25

The florist should put 15 flowers in each vase.

Jacob's method

```
        1   5
  5 ) 7   5
    -  5   0
       2   5
    -  2   5
           0
```

I prefer to divide this way because I can see all the steps.

Hannah's method

I like dividing this way.
I have to do the steps in my head
and I write less things down.

$$\begin{array}{r} 1 \quad\ 5 \\ 5\overline{\smash{)}7\ _2 5} \end{array}$$

5 goes into 7 one time.
I write a 1 above the line in the tens column.
I then subtract. 7 tens − 5 tens = 2 tens
I then write the remaining
2 tens next to the ones.

I can see 2 tens and 5 ones are left.
25 ÷ 5 = 5
I then write the 5 above the line in
the ones column.

Practice

Use Hannah's method to divide.

1 96 ÷ 6 = ☐

$$6\overline{\smash{)}9\quad 6}$$

2 91 ÷ 7 = ☐

$$7\overline{\smash{)}9\quad 1}$$

3 85 ÷ 5 = ☐

$$5\overline{\smash{)}8\quad 5}$$

4 75 ÷ 5 = ☐

$$5\overline{\smash{)}7\quad 5}$$

5 96 ÷ 4 = ☐

$$4\overline{\smash{)}9\quad 6}$$

6 94 ÷ 2 = ☐

$$2\overline{\smash{)}9\quad 4}$$

Review and challenge

 1 Solve and fill in the blanks.

(a) 3 × 7 = ☐

(b) 3 × 4 = ☐

(c) 3 × 3 = ☐

(d) 8 × 3 = ☐

(e)

There are ☐ groups of ☐ .

3 × ☐ = ☐

(f)

There are ☐ rows of ☐ .

☐ × ☐ = ☐

2 Solve and fill in the blanks.

(a) 4 × 9 = ⬜

(b) 4 × 8 = ⬜

(c) 4 × 5 = ⬜

(d) 7 × 4 = ⬜

(e)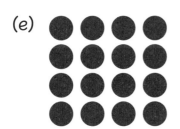

There are ⬜ rows of ⬜ .

⬜ × ⬜ = ⬜

(f)

There are ⬜ rows of ⬜ .

⬜ × ⬜ = ⬜

3 Match.

4 × 8 ●	● 16
5 × 8 ●	● 8
10 × 8 ●	● 24
2 × 8 ●	● 32
9 × 8 ●	● 40
1 × 8 ●	● 64
8 × 8 ●	● 56
3 × 8 ●	● 72
7 × 8 ●	● 80

4 Solve.

(a) $27 \div 3 =$ ☐

(b) $30 \div$ ☐ $= 3$

(c) $32 \div 4 =$ ☐

(d) $32 \div 8 =$ ☐

5 (a) Circle to show groups of 4 and fill in the blank.

(b) Circle to show groups of 8 and fill in the blanks.

$40 \div 4 =$ ☐

$40 \div$ ☐ $=$ ☐

(c) Circle to show 4 groups and fill in the blanks.

$\boxed{} \div 4 = \boxed{}$

(d) Circle to show 8 groups and fill in the blanks.

$\boxed{} \div 8 = \boxed{}$

6 Solve and fill in the blanks.

(a) $68 \div 4 = \boxed{}$

$$
\begin{array}{r}
\boxed{}\,\boxed{} \\
4\,)\,\overline{\quad 6 \quad 8} \\
-\,\boxed{}\,\boxed{} \\
\hline
\boxed{}\,\boxed{} \\
-\,\boxed{}\,\boxed{} \\
\hline
0
\end{array}
$$

(b) $57 \div 3 = \boxed{}$

$$
\begin{array}{r}
\boxed{}\,\boxed{} \\
3\,)\,\overline{\quad 5 \quad 7} \\
-\,\boxed{}\,\boxed{} \\
\hline
\boxed{}\,\boxed{} \\
-\,\boxed{}\,\boxed{} \\
\hline
0
\end{array}
$$

7 Ravi's cat weighs 4 kg. His dog weighs twice as much as his cat.
Ravi weighs three times as much as his dog.

4 kg

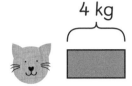

(a) How much does Ravi's dog weigh?

4 × ☐ = ☐ kg

Ravi's dog weighs ☐ kg.

(b) How much does Ravi weigh?

4 × ☐ = ☐ kg

Ravi weighs ☐ kg.

(c) How much do Ravi, his dog and his cat weigh altogether?

4 × ☐ = ☐ kg

Ravi, his dog and his cat weigh ☐ kg altogether.

Answers

Page 5   **1 (a)** 3 × 2 = 6, 3 × 4 = 12 **(b)** 3 × 3 = 9 **(c)** 3 × 5 = 15

Page 6   **2** 3 groups of 3

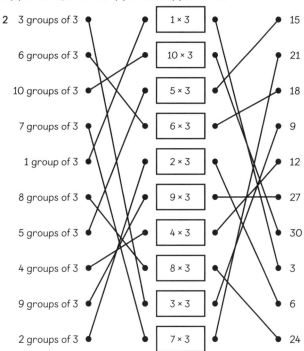

Page 7   **3 (a)** The baker bakes 12 loaves in the morning. **(b)** The baker bakes 15 loaves in the afternoon.
(c) The baker bakes 27 loaves altogether.

Page 9   **1 (b)** 2 × 4 = 8 **(c)** 3 × 4 = 12 **(d)** 4 × 4 = 16 **(e)** 5 × 4 = 20 **(f)** 6 × 4 = 24 **(g)** 7 × 4 = 28 **(h)** 8 × 4 = 32 **(i)** 9 × 4 = 36 **(j)** 10 × 4 = 40

Page 10   **2** 4 × 10 = 40. There are 40 drinks altogether. **3** There are 24 kitchen rolls in 4 packs.

Page 11   **4** Elliott has 20 pencils.   **5**

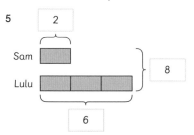

2 × 4 = 8. Sam and Lulu read 8 books in total last term.

Page 13   **1 (a)** 4 × 8 = 32 **(b)** 3 × 8 = 24 **(c)** 1 × 8 = 8 **(d)** 5 × 8 = 40 **(e)** 8 × 8 = 64 **(f)** 8 × 10 = 80 **(g)** 7 × 8 = 56 **(h)** 9 × 8 = 72 **(i)** 2 × 8 = 16 **(j)** 6 × 8 = 48

2

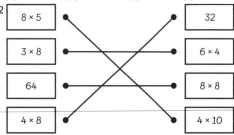

Page 15   **1 (a)**   **(b)**

27 ÷ 3 = 9. There are 9 groups of 3 counters.   21 ÷ 3 = 7. There are 7 stars in each group.

2 (a) 21 ÷ 3 = 7 **(b)** 15 ÷ 3 = 5 **(c)** 30 ÷ 3 = 10 **(d)** 18 ÷ 3 = 6 **3** Oak needs 8 plates. **4** Each piece of fabric will be 9 m long.

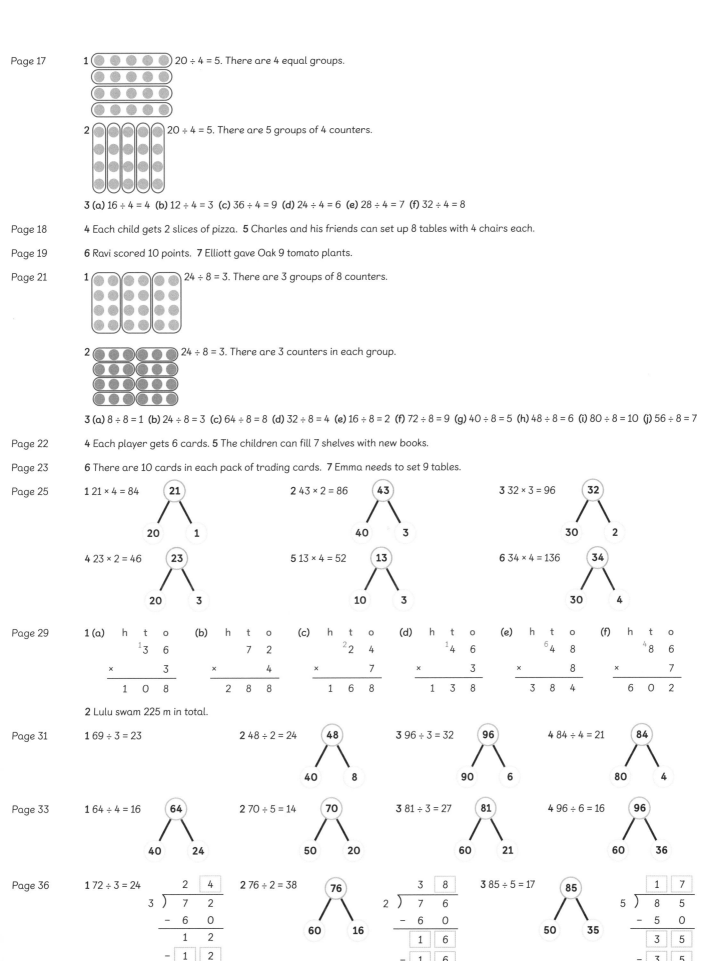

Page 17   1 $20 ÷ 4 = 5$. There are 4 equal groups.

2 $20 ÷ 4 = 5$. There are 5 groups of 4 counters.

3 (a) $16 ÷ 4 = 4$ (b) $12 ÷ 4 = 3$ (c) $36 ÷ 4 = 9$ (d) $24 ÷ 4 = 6$ (e) $28 ÷ 4 = 7$ (f) $32 ÷ 4 = 8$

Page 18   4 Each child gets 2 slices of pizza. 5 Charles and his friends can set up 8 tables with 4 chairs each.

Page 19   6 Ravi scored 10 points. 7 Elliott gave Oak 9 tomato plants.

Page 21   1 $24 ÷ 8 = 3$. There are 3 groups of 8 counters.

2 $24 ÷ 8 = 3$. There are 3 counters in each group.

3 (a) $8 ÷ 8 = 1$ (b) $24 ÷ 8 = 3$ (c) $64 ÷ 8 = 8$ (d) $32 ÷ 8 = 4$ (e) $16 ÷ 8 = 2$ (f) $72 ÷ 8 = 9$ (g) $40 ÷ 8 = 5$ (h) $48 ÷ 8 = 6$ (i) $80 ÷ 8 = 10$ (j) $56 ÷ 8 = 7$

Page 22   4 Each player gets 6 cards. 5 The children can fill 7 shelves with new books.

Page 23   6 There are 10 cards in each pack of trading cards. 7 Emma needs to set 9 tables.

Page 25   1 $21 × 4 = 84$ **21** = **20** **1**
   2 $43 × 2 = 86$ **43** = **40** **3**
   3 $32 × 3 = 96$ **32** = **30** **2**

4 $23 × 2 = 46$ **23** = **20** **3**
   5 $13 × 4 = 52$ **13** = **10** **3**
   6 $34 × 4 = 136$ **34** = **30** **4**

Page 29   1 (a) $\begin{array}{ccc} h & t & o \\ & ^13 & 6 \\ × & & 3 \\ \hline 1 & 0 & 8 \end{array}$ (b) $\begin{array}{ccc} h & t & o \\ & 7 & 2 \\ × & & 4 \\ \hline 2 & 8 & 8 \end{array}$ (c) $\begin{array}{ccc} h & t & o \\ & ^22 & 4 \\ × & & 7 \\ \hline 1 & 6 & 8 \end{array}$ (d) $\begin{array}{ccc} h & t & o \\ & ^14 & 6 \\ × & & 3 \\ \hline 1 & 3 & 8 \end{array}$ (e) $\begin{array}{ccc} h & t & o \\ & ^64 & 8 \\ × & & 8 \\ \hline 3 & 8 & 4 \end{array}$ (f) $\begin{array}{ccc} h & t & o \\ & ^48 & 6 \\ × & & 7 \\ \hline 6 & 0 & 2 \end{array}$

2 Lulu swam 225 m in total.

Page 31   1 $69 ÷ 3 = 23$ 2 $48 ÷ 2 = 24$ **48** = **40** **8**   3 $96 ÷ 3 = 32$ **96** = **90** **6**   4 $84 ÷ 4 = 21$ **84** = **80** **4**

Page 33   1 $64 ÷ 4 = 16$ **64** = **40** **24**   2 $70 ÷ 5 = 14$ **70** = **50** **20**   3 $81 ÷ 3 = 27$ **81** = **60** **21**   4 $96 ÷ 6 = 16$ **96** = **60** **36**

Page 36   1 $72 ÷ 3 = 24$
$\begin{array}{r} 2\ \boxed{4} \\ 3\ )\ 7\ \ 2 \\ -\ 6\ \ 0 \\ \hline 1\ \ 2 \\ -\ \boxed{1}\ \boxed{2} \\ \hline 0 \end{array}$

2 $76 ÷ 2 = 38$ **76** = **60** **16**

$\begin{array}{r} 3\ \boxed{8} \\ 2\ )\ 7\ \ 6 \\ -\ 6\ \ 0 \\ \hline \boxed{1}\ \boxed{6} \\ -\ 1\ \ 6 \\ \hline 0 \end{array}$

3 $85 ÷ 5 = 17$ **85** = **50** **35**

$\begin{array}{r} \boxed{1}\ \boxed{7} \\ 5\ )\ 8\ \ 5 \\ -\ 5\ \ 0 \\ \hline 3\ \ 5 \\ -\ 3\ \ 5 \\ \hline 0 \end{array}$

Answers continued

Page 37 **4** $87 \div 3 = 29$

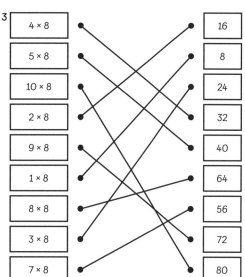

5 Sam is 9 years old and his brother is 5 years old.

Page 39 **1** $96 \div 6 = 16$

$$6 \overline{)\ 9\ {}_3 6} \quad \begin{smallmatrix}1 & 6\end{smallmatrix}$$

2 $91 \div 7 = 13$

$$7 \overline{)\ 9\ {}_2 1} \quad \begin{smallmatrix}1 & 3\end{smallmatrix}$$

3 $85 \div 5 = 17$

$$5 \overline{)\ 8\ {}_3 5} \quad \begin{smallmatrix}1 & 7\end{smallmatrix}$$

4 $75 \div 5 = 15$

$$5 \overline{)\ 7\ {}_2 5} \quad \begin{smallmatrix}1 & 5\end{smallmatrix}$$

5 $96 \div 4 = 24$

$$4 \overline{)\ 9\ {}_1 6} \quad \begin{smallmatrix}2 & 4\end{smallmatrix}$$

6 $94 \div 2 = 47$

$$2 \overline{)\ 9\ {}_1 4} \quad \begin{smallmatrix}4 & 7\end{smallmatrix}$$

Page 40 **1 (a)** $3 \times 7 = 21$ **(b)** $3 \times 4 = 12$ **(c)** $3 \times 3 = 9$ **(d)** $8 \times 3 = 24$ **(e)** There are 4 groups of 3. $3 \times 4 = 12$ **(f)** There are 5 rows of 3. $3 \times 5 = 15$

Page 41 **2 (a)** $4 \times 9 = 36$ **(b)** $4 \times 8 = 32$ **(c)** $4 \times 5 = 20$ **(d)** $7 \times 4 = 28$ **(e)** There are 4 rows of 4. $4 \times 4 = 16$ **(f)** There are 9 rows of 5. $9 \times 5 = 45$

Page 42 **3**

4 × 8	16
5 × 8	8
10 × 8	24
2 × 8	32
9 × 8	40
1 × 8	64
8 × 8	56
3 × 8	72
7 × 8	80

Page 43 **4 (a)** $27 \div 3 = 9$ **(b)** $30 \div 10 = 3$ **(c)** $32 \div 4 = 8$ **(d)** $32 \div 8 = 4$

5 (a)

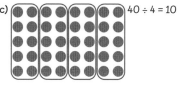

$40 \div 4 = 10$

(b) $40 \div 5 = 8$

Page 44 **(c)** $40 \div 4 = 10$

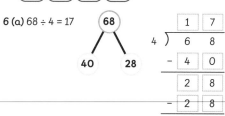

(d) $40 \div 8 = 5$

6 (a) $68 \div 4 = 17$

(b) $57 \div 3 = 19$

Page 45 **7 (a)** $4 \times 2 = 8$ kg. Ravi's dog weighs 8 kg. **(b)** $4 \times 6 = 24$ kg. Ravi weighs 24 kg. **(c)** $4 \times 9 = 36$ kg. Ravi, his dog and his cat weigh 36 kg altogether.